GALE
CENGAGE Learning

Novels for Students, Volume 10

Staff

Series Editors: Michael L. LaBlanc and Ira Mark Milne.

Contributing Editors: Elizabeth Bellalouna, Elizabeth Bodenmiller, Reginald Carlton, Anne Marie Hacht, Polly Rapp, Jennifer Smith.

Research: Victoria B. Cariappa, *Research Team Manager*. Maureen Eremic, Barb McNeil, Cheryl Warnock, *Research Specialists*. Andy Malonis, *Technical Training Specialist*. Barbara Leevy, Tamara Nott, Tracie A. Richardson, Robert Whaley, *Research Associates*. Scott Floyd, Nicodemus Ford, Sarah Genik, Timothy Lehnerer, *Research Assistants*.

Permissions: Maria Franklin, *Permissions Manager*. Margaret A. Chamberlain, Edna Hedblad, *Permissions Specialists*. Erin Bealmear, Shalice Shah-Caldwell, Sarah Tomasek, *Permissions*

Associates. Debra Freitas, Julie Juengling, Mark Plaza, *Permissions Assistants.*

Manufacturing: Mary Beth Trimper, *Manager, Composition and Electronic Prepress.* Evi Seoud, *Assistant Manager, Composition Purchasing and Electronic Prepress.* Stacy Melson, *Buyer.*

Imaging and Multimedia Content Team: Randy Bassett, *Image Database Supervisor.* Robert Duncan, Dan Newell, *Imaging Specialists.* Pamela A. Reed, *Imaging Coordinator.* Dean Dauphinais, Robyn V. Young, *Senior Image Editors.* Kelly A. Quin, *Image Editor.*

Product Design Team: Kenn Zorn, *Product Design Manager.* Pamela A. E. Galbreath, *Senior Art Director.* Michael Logusz, *Graphic Artist.*

Copyright Notice

of the publisher and verified to the satisfaction of the publisher will be corrected in future editions.

This publication is a creative work fully protected by all applicable copyright laws, as well as by misappropriation, trade secret, unfair competition, and other applicable laws. The authors and editors of this work have added value to the underlying factual material herein through one or more of the following: unique and original selection, coordination, expression, arrangement, and classification of the information. All rights to this publication will be vigorously defended.

Copyright © 2001
Gale Group
27500 Drake Rd.
Farmington Hills, MI 48331-3535

ISBN 0-7876-3829-3
ISSN 1094-3552

Printed in the United States of America.
10 9 8 7 6 5 4 3 2 1

Chronicle of a Death Foretold

Gabriel García Márquez
1982

Introduction

Gabriel García Márquez's novel *Chronicle of a Death Foretold*, first published in English in 1982, is one of the Nobel Prizewinning author's shorter novels, but past and current critics agree that the book's small size hides a huge work of art. According to Jonathan Yardley in *Washington Post Book World*, *Chronicle of a Death Foretold* "is, in miniature, a virtuoso performance."

The book's power lies in the unique way in which García Márquez relates the plot of a murder about which everyone knows before it happens. A narrator tells the story in the first person, as a witness to the events that occurred. Yet the narrator is recounting the tale years later from an omniscient point of view, sharing all of the characters' thoughts. García Márquez's use of this creative technique adds to the mystery of the murder. In addition, the repeated foretelling of the crime helps build the suspense. Even though the murderers' identities are known, the specific details of the killing are not.

Besides its unusual point of view, the book's themes also contribute to its success. The question of male honor in Latin American culture underlies this story of passion and crime. As in other García Márquez works, there is also an element of the supernatural: dreams and other mystical signs ominously portend the murder. García Márquez's artistry in combining these elements led critic Edith Grossman to say in *Review*, "Once again García Márquez is an ironic chronicler who dazzles the reader with uncommon blendings of fantasy, fable, and fact."

Author Biography

Best known as the author of the prizewinning *One Hundred Years of Solitude*, Gabriel García Márquez began life in Aracataca, Colombia, on March 6, 1928. The son of poor parents, Gabriel Eligio Garcia and Luisa Santiaga Márquez Iguarán, García Márquez lived with his grandparents for the first eight years of his life. According to Márquez, this is a common practice in the Caribbean. In his case, though, his grandparents offered to raise him as a reconciliatory gesture towards their daughter after opposing her marriage to García Márquez's father. As a result, García Márquez grew up in a house with his grandparents, aunts, and uncles and hardly knew his mother. His extended family regaled him with stories: the women told tales of superstition and fantasy, while the men—especially his grandfather—kept him grounded in reality.

In 1947, García Márquez entered the National University of Colombia, in Bogota, to study law. He had to transfer to the University of Cartagena when civil war erupted and closed the University of Bogota. There he began his work as a journalist. He dropped out of college to work as a reporter for the daily paper, *El heraldo*, in Barranquilla and began writing short stories. He had published his first short story, "The Third Resignation," in 1946. The editor of the Bogota newspaper that had published it, *El Espectador* hailed García Márquez as the "new genius of Colombian letters." García Márquez himself, however, was not satisfied with his writing, until a visit back to Aracataca, which was, according to García Márquez, a crucial turning point in his writing. He said in a 1983 *Playboy* interview with Claudia Dreifus, "That day, I realized that all the short stories I had written to that point were simply intellectual elaborations, nothing to do with my reality." García Márquez's writing from that point on reflects the influences of his grandmother's storytelling as well as the myths, superstitions, and lifestyle of the people in Aracataca. *Leaf Storm* introduced the fictional setting, Ma-condo (named for a banana plantation he saw on his trip back to Aracataca), and its inhabitants. Reviewers think the setting resembles William Faulkner's Yoknapatawpha County.

Even though García Márquez started his most celebrated novel, *One Hundred Years of Solitude*, when he was only twenty, he did not feel that he knew what he really wanted to say in it until about thirteen years later. García Márquez says in the *Playboy* interview that he was driving to Acapulco when he suddenly had an "illumination" of the tone and everything in the story. Upon his return home, he began writing for six hours a day over the next eighteen months. His wife, Mercedes—whom he married in 1958—cared for their two young sons and supported him.

The resulting book established García Márquez as "one of the greatest living storytellers," according to *Time* magazine correspondent R. Z. Sheppard. He has written several critically acclaimed novels and short stories since then. *Chronicle of a Death Foretold*, published in English in 1982, further developed his reputation as political novelist, and he later wrote both fictionalized and nonfiction accounts of Latin American history. García Márquez's works have won numerous awards, including the 1982 Nobel Prize for Literature.

Plot Summary

Chronicle of a Death Foretold relates the events leading up to and, to a lesser degree, those that follow the murder of Santiago Nasar, a twenty-one year old Colombian of Arab descent. He is killed by the Vicario brothers to avenge the loss of their sister's honor. Told twenty-seven years after the crime by an unnamed narrator (arguably García Márquez himself) who returns to the village where he once lived to put back together "the broken mirror of memory," the story is constructed from the fragmented and often conflicting versions of events as they are remembered by the townspeople and by the narrator himself.

Chapter 1

On the morning after the wedding celebrations for Angela Vicario and Bayardo San Román, Santiago Nasar, son of Plácida Linero and the late Ibrahim Nasar, wakes to greet the bishop who is arriving by boat early that morning. When he enters the kitchen, both the cook, Victoria Guzmán, and her daughter, Divina Flora, know what Santiago Nasar will not learn for some time—that two men are waiting outside the house to kill him. They, like many others Santiago will cross in the short time before his death, do not warn him.

When Santiago leaves the house, he passes the milk shop owned by Clotilde Armenta where the twins, Pedro and Pablo Vicario, are waiting to kill him. It is Clotilde Armenta's plea to "leave him for later, if only out of respect for his grace the bishop" that keeps the twins from killing him immediately. The bishop, however, never gets off his boat and departs after drifting past the crowd gathered on the pier. Santiago then joins Margot, the narrator's sister, and their friend Cristo Bedoya, two of the only people who still do not know about the twins' intentions. Santiago accepts an invitation to breakfast with Margot but wishes first to return home and change.

Meanwhile, Margot learns that Angela Vicario has been returned to her parents by her husband because he discovered that she wasn't a virgin. She does not know how Santiago is involved, only that two men are waiting for him to kill him. When Margot's (and the narrator's) mother hears the news, she immediately sets out to warn Plácida Linero that her son is in danger, but is stopped in the street and told that "they've already killed him."

Chapter 2

Bayardo San Román arrived in the town for the first time in August of the year before looking for someone to marry. According to the narrator, it was never well established how he and Angela Vicario met. One version has Bayardo deciding to marry Angela after first seeing her pass by his boarding house; another has the pair meeting for the first time on the national holiday in October. According to the latter version, Bayardo wins a music box which he has gift-wrapped and delivered to Angela's home. He soon wins the family with his charms and, despite Angela's protests, succeeds in making her his fiancée.

Prior to the wedding, Angela comes close to telling her mother that she isn't a virgin but is dissuaded from her good intentions and follows the advice of two confidantes who teach her how "to feign her lost possession" so that, on her first morning as a newlywed, she can display the sheet with the stain of honor. When her wedding night arrives, however, she is unable to carry out the "dirty" trick and is returned to her parents' house by her husband. At home, Angela is beaten by her mother and is confronted by her brothers, to whom she reveals the name of the man responsible: Santiago Nasar.

Chapter 3

After completing their gruesome task, the Vicario brothers surrender themselves to their church and announce that although they killed Santiago Nasar openly, they are innocent because it was a matter of honor. Despite their lack of remorse, the narrator tries to demonstrate that the twins did all they could to have someone stop them.

In the meat market where the twins go to sharpen their knives, Pedro and Pablo take every opportunity to announce their intentions. "We're going to kill Santiago Nasar," they say repeatedly.

Later, at Clotilde Armenta's, they even reveal their plans to a policeman who passes on the information to the mayor. The latter takes away the twins' knives, but Clotilde Armenta believes the twins should be detained to spare them "from the horrible duty that's fallen on them." She says this knowing that the Vicario brothers are "not as eager to carry out the sentence as to find someone who would do them the favor of stopping them."

Although Pedro thinks his and his brother's duty fulfilled when the mayor disarms them, Pablo insists they carry out their deed. "There's no way out of this," Pablo tells his brother, "it's as if it had already happened." They return to Clotilde Armenta's with a new set of knives and wait while "fake customers" come in to see whether what they have heard is true.

Chapter 4

Following Santiago Nasar's death, an autopsy is performed and determines that the cause of death was a massive hemorrhage brought on by any one of seven major wounds. The autopsy, a "massacre" performed by Father Amador in the absence of Dr. Dionosio Iguarán, makes it impossible to preserve the body and Santiago is buried hurriedly at dawn the next day.

On that day too the entire Vicario family, except the imprisoned twins, leaves town "until spirits cool off." They never return. The twins remain imprisoned for three years awaiting their trial but are eventually absolved of the crime. Pablo then marries his longtime fiancée and Pedro re-enlists in the armed forces and disappears in guerrilla territory.

For many, the only real victim in this tragedy is Bayardo San Román. He is found in his home on the Saturday following the crime, unconscious and in the last stages of ethylic intoxication. He recovers and is later taken away by his family. Angela, for her part, goes "crazy" for her husband following her rejection on her wedding night. For years she writes him a weekly letter until, one day, he shows up at her door, fat and balding, but wearing the same belt and saddlebags he wore in his youth. He carries with him a suitcase with clothing in order to stay and another filled with the almost two thousand unopened letters that she'd written him.

Chapter 5

According to the narrator, Santiago Nasar dies without understanding his death. It is only after parting from Margot and Cristo Bedoya, when Santiago enters the home of his fiancée, Flora Miguel, that he is finally told that the Vicario brothers are waiting for him to kill him. Flora Miguel has heard the news and, fearing that Santiago will be forced to marry Angela Vicario to give her back her honor, returns to him his letters, crying, "I hope they kill you."

When Santiago leaves his fiancée's house, confused and disoriented, he finds himself amid crowds of people stationed on the square as they do on parade days. He begins to walk towards his house and is spotted by the twins. Clotilde Armenta yells to Santiago to run, but Santiago's mother, believing that her son is already up in his room, locks the door seconds before he would have reached safety. Instead, the twins catch up to him and carve him with their knives. The watching crowd shouts, "frightened by its own crime." When the twins are done, Santiago is left "holding his hanging intestines in his hands," walks more than a hundred yards to the back door of his house and falls on his face in the kitchen.

Colonel Aponte

See Lazaro Aponte

Lazaro Aponte

The head of the police, Lazaro Aponte (also known as Colonel Aponte) first hears of the twins' plot to kill Santiago a little after four o'clock that morning. He has just finished shaving when one of his officers, Leandro Pornoy, tells him. He does not take the threat too seriously, because when he sees the twins, they seem fairly sober. He takes their knives away and feels assured that they will not carry out their plan.

Clotilde Armenta

Owner of the milk shop where the killers slept and awaited Santiago, Clotilde Armenta claims that Santiago already looked like a ghost when she saw him early on the morning of the murder. She makes a mild attempt to convince the twins not to kill Santiago.

Cristo Bedoya

Cristo is a friend of Santiago and of the

narrator. The three young men spend the night before the murder attending Angela Vicario's wedding. The next morning, Cristo is with Margot and Santiago on the pier awaiting the bishop's arrival. Cristo and Santiago go their separate ways when they reach the village square. When Cristo hears of the murder plot, he tries, to no avail, to catch up with Santiago to warn him.

Maria Cervantes

Maria owns the brothel, or "house of mercies," where Santiago Nasar, Cristo Bedoya, Luis Enrique, and his brother, the narrator, continue their partying after the wedding. Maria has the reputation of having helped all of them lose their virginity. She is tender and beautiful, yet strict about her house rules.

Purisima del Carmen

Purisima is the mother of Angela and the twins, Pedro and Pablo. A former schoolteacher, Purisima is married to Poncio and has dedicated her life to being a wife and mother. She has raised her daughters to be good wives and mothers and her sons to be men.

Divina Flor

A young woman just entering adolescence, Divina Flor is Victoria Guzmán's daughter. Seeing Santiago always overwhelms Divina with emotions she can not yet define. Santiago touches her in ways she does not like and seems to want to harm her. She knows of the plot to kill Santiago, but like her mother, she tells him nothing. She is too young to decide to tell him on her own and is frightened enough by him to want to keep her distance.

Victoria Guzmán

Victoria Guzmán cooks for the Nasar family. Formerly Ibrahim Nasar's mistress, Victoria views Santiago with as much disdain as she does his late father. She still hates Ibrahim for keeping her as his mistress and then making her his cook when he tired of her. She thinks Santiago is exactly like his father and works diligently to keep Santiago away from her daughter, Divina Flor. Victoria learns early on the morning of the murder that Santiago is destined to die, but she says nothing to him.

Plácida Linero

Santiago's mother, Plácida Linero, interprets people's dreams. On the day of her son's death, however, she fails to recognize the significance of Santiago's dream of birds and trees the night before. She regrets that she paid more attention to the birds, which signify good health. Trees, on the other hand, are an omen. In her later years, Plácida suffers from chronic headaches that started on the day she last saw her son. Her knowledge that she unwittingly closed the main door of the house against Santiago, where his killers caught up with him, haunts her.

Flora Miguel

Flora is Santiago's fiancée through their parents' arrangement. Her family never opens the doors or receives visitors before noon. Flora learns early on the morning of the murder that Santiago is going to die. Because she is afraid that if Santiago lives he will have to marry Angela to save her honor, Flora invites Santiago into her home and vents her frustration and rage. Flora's father, concerned about his daughter, comes to check on her and is the one who tells Santiago of the plot.

Narrator

The narrator never gives his name, but he is a member of the Santiaga family, son to Luisa and brother to Margot. He is also a friend of Santiago Nasar. The narrator has returned to his village twenty-seven years after Santiago's murder and is trying to piece together the events of the day.

Ibrahim Nasar

Ibrahim Nasar, Santiago's father and Plácida Linero's husband, has been dead for three years when the story opens. His memory lives on in Santiago, however, who has his good looks and runs his ranch. Nasar had come to the Caribbean village with the last group of Arabs who arrived after the civil wars ended. A relatively wealthy man, he had purchased the warehouse—in which Plácida and Santiago live—and brought his mistress, Victoria

Guzmán, to live with them as their cook. Victoria despises Ibrahim for his womanizing and hates Santiago because he so much behaves like his father.

Santiago Nasar

The son of the recently deceased Arab, Ibrahim Nasar, Santiago Nasar lives with his mother, Plácida Linero, in a small Caribbean village. Twenty-one-year-old Santiago resembles his father. He has his father's Arab eyelids and curly hair. He also possesses his father's love for horses and firearms as well as his wisdom and values. Having inherited the family ranch, The Divine Face, Santiago enjoys a comfortable life and has money to spare. From his mother, Santiago has received a sixth sense about things. On the day of his death, Santiago tells his mother of dreams that he has been having about trees and birds.

Media Adaptations

- Graciela Daniele adapted *Chronicle of a Death Foretold* as an on-Broadway musical performed at the Plymouth Theater in New York City in July, 1995. The theater production received mixed reviews, but was nominated for a Tony award in the Best Musical category.

Slim and pale, Santiago wears his clothes well —typically a khaki outfit and boots when he is working. On special occasions, such as the day of the Bishop's arrival at the beginning of the story, Santiago looks especially handsome in his white linen shirt and pants. Women appreciate Santiago's good looks and fortune as well as his pleasant disposition. They consider him a man of his word. Men, too, admire Santiago. When his father dies, Santiago has to leave his studies to manage the family business, yet he never complains and is always willing to join with his friends in celebrations of any kind. They know Santiago to be a man who is careful with his guns and ammunition and who has no reason to arm himself except when he is working in the country.

Santiago is to marry Flora Miguel at Christmas time. He seems happy with the arrangement and is content to live life as it is. He appears to have no enemies. Santiago's happy-go-lucky lifestyle ends, however, when Angela Vicario accuses him of taking her virginity.

Pura

See Purisima Del Carmen

Bayardo San Román

The insulted bridegroom Bayardo San Román returns Angela Vicario to her parents' home when he discovers that she is not a virgin. San Román acts very much the gentleman whom people have come to know since he appeared in their small community. Having only been a resident for six months, San Román still has people guessing about his background. The women, however, love his looks and do not worry about who he is. He arrives dressed in a short calfskin jacket, tight trousers, and gloves to match, with silver decorating his boots, belt, and saddlebags. His physique matches that of a bullfighter's, and his skin glows with health. When Bayardo's family arrives for the wedding, the townspeople discover that Bayardo is the son of a wealthy civil war hero.

General Petronio San Román

Bayardo's father, the General, arrives for the wedding in a Model T Ford with an official license. Famous for his leadership in the past century's civil wars, he is immediately recognizable. The General wears the Medal of Valor on his jacket and carries a cane that bears the nation shield. The people of the village no longer question Bayardo's honor and understand that because of who he is, Bayardo can marry anyone.

Luisa Santiaga

Luisa, the narrator's mother, typically knows everything that is going on. On the morning of the killing, however, she goes about her business at home without any inkling of Santiago's fate. When her daughter, Margot, arrives home and begins to relate what she has heard on the docks, however, Luisa suddenly knows before Margot has finished telling her. Luisa is Santiago's godmother but is also a blood relative of Pura Vicario, Angela's mother; therefore, the knowledge of the plan to kill Santiago poses a problem for Luisa.

Margot Santiaga

The narrator's sister and Luisa's daughter, Margot envies Santiago's fiancée. To spend time with Santiago, Margot often invites Santiago to breakfast at her parents' home. Having felt a premonition about Santiago on the day of the murder, she urges Santiago to go home with her immediately. Later, she learns about the plot to kill Santiago while she is awaiting the arrival of the bishop. She is distressed by the news and hurries home to tell her mother.

Angela Vicario

The sister to twins Pedro and Pablo, Angela suffers great humiliation when her newlywed husband discovers that she is not a virgin. Angela is the youngest daughter of the Vicario family, who have raised her to marry. Even though she is prettier than her sisters, she somewhat resembles a nun, appearing meek and helpless. The Vicarios have watched over her carefully, so Angela has had little chance to develop social skills or to be alone with men. Everyone expects Angela to be chaste. When they discover Angela's secret, the family reacts violently to the knowledge that Santiago Nasar is responsible for her disgrace.

Pablo Vicario

Even though twenty-four-year-old Pablo is the older of the Vicario twins by about six minutes, he assumes the role of the obliging younger brother. When Pedro leaves for the military, Pablo stays home to mind the business and take care of the family. Upon Pedro's return, however, Pablo is happy to depend on his brother's leadership. Pedro claims the responsibility for making the decision to kill Santiago. Pablo, however, actually gets the knives and convinces Pedro to carry out his plans after the mayor has disarmed them once.

Pedro Vicario

Pedro Vicario, pig slaughterer by trade, is the

twin to Pablo. Pedro and Pablo are responsible for Santiago's murder. Pedro is the "younger" of the twins, having been born about six minutes after Pablo. Twenty-four years old, Pedro and Pablo have lived a hard life. They have a reputation for heavy drinking and carousing. Pedro started their slaughtering business after his father lost his eyesight. While Pedro is the more sensitive of the two, his time in the military has made him hard. He likes to give people orders. Pedro claims to have made the decision to kill Santiago. In addition to acquiring in the military his tendency to command, Pedro also contracted blennorrhea, a medical condition that makes urination difficult and painful.

Poncio Vicario

Poncio Vicario heads the Vicario household. As a former goldsmith who spent years doing close work, he has lost his eyesight. While the family still holds him in high esteem, he is not accustomed to being blind and appears confused and anxious most of the time.

The Widower Xius

Bayardo convinces the widower Xius, an old man living alone in the prettiest house in town, to sell it. He does not decide to relinquish his home, though, until Bayardo offers him ten thousand pesos. Although extremely sentimental about his home and unhappy to be put in such a position, the widower gives in. He dies only two months later.

Honor

The motive for the murder of Santiago Nasar lies undetected until halfway through *Chronicle of a Death Foretold*. While everyone knows that Nasar will be murdered, no one knows the reason. Then, after a night of carousing, the Vicario twins, Pedro and Pablo, return home at their mother's summons. The family presses a devastated Angela, the twins' sister, to tell the reason for her humiliated return from her marriage bed. When Angela says, "Santiago Nasar," the twins know immediately that they must defend their sister's honor. The twins' attorney views the act as "homicide in legitimate defense of honor," which is upheld by the court. The priest calls the twins' surrender "an act of great dignity." When the twins claim their innocence, the priest says that they may be so before God, while Pablo Vicario says, "Before God and before men. It was a matter of honor."

Revenge

While the twins say the murder was necessary for their sister's good name, and the courts agree with them, many disagree, viewing the murder as a cruel act of revenge. The manner in which they kill Santiago appears to be much more vicious than what a simple murder for honor would entail. The twins first obtain their two best butchering knives, one for quartering and one for trimming. When Colonel Aponte takes these knives from them, the twins return to their butchering shop to get another quartering knife—with a broad, curved blade—and a twelve-inch knife with a rusty edge. Intent on making sure Santiago is dead, the twins use the knives to stab him over and over again. Seven of the wounds are fatal; the liver, stomach, pancreas, and colon are nearly destroyed. The twins stab him with such vengeance that they are covered with blood themselves, and the main door of Plácida Linero's house, where Santiago was killed, must be repaired by the city. Further supporting the view that the twins acted in revenge is the fact that they show no remorse for the murder.

After the murder, the twins fear revenge from the Arab community. Even though they believe they have rightfully murdered Santiago for their sister's honor, the twins think that the tightly knit community of Arabs will seek revenge for the loss of one of their own. When Pablo becomes ill at the jail, Pedro is convinced that the Arabs have poisoned him.

Sex Roles

Purisima del Carmen, Angela Vicario's mother, has raised her daughters to be good wives. The girls do not marry until late in life, seldom socializing beyond the confines of their own home. They spend their time doing embroidery, sewing, weaving, washing and ironing, arranging flowers, making candy, and writing engagement announcements. They also keep the old traditions alive, such as sitting up with the ill, comforting the dying, and enshrouding the dead. While their mother believes they are perfect, men view them as too tied to their women's traditions.

Purisima del Carmen's sons, on the other hand, are raised to be men. They serve in the war, take over their father's business when he goes blind, drink and party until all hours of the night, and spend time in the local brothel. When the family insists on Angela's marrying Bayardo, a man she has seldom even seen, the twins stay out of it because, "It looked to us like woman problems." "Woman problems" become "men's problems" when the family calls the twins home upon Angela's return. She feels relieved to let them take the matter into their hands, as the family expects them to do.

Deception

Angela Vicario is not a virgin when she marries Bayardo, but no one would suspect otherwise. Her mother has sheltered her for her entire life. Angela has never been engaged before, nor has she been allowed to go out alone with Bayardo in the time they have known one another. Angela, however, is concerned that her bridegroom will learn her secret on their wedding night, and considers telling her mother before the wedding. Instead, she tells two of her friends, who advise her not to tell her mother. In addition, they tell Angela that men do not really know the difference and that she can trick Bayardo into believing that she is a virgin. Angela believes them. Not only does Angela wear the veil and orange blossoms that signify purity, she carries out her friends' plan of deception on her wedding night.

Topics for Further Study

- Pedro Vicario suffers from a medical condition he acquired while in the military. What is the condition? Research its causes, symptoms, and treatments. Assume the role of a medical practitioner and create a presentation to inform your colleagues about the illness.

- In *Chronicle of a Death Foretold*, the narrator tells the story from a first-person omniscient point of view. Study the various literary points of view and explain why this is an unusual technique.

- Literary critics often credit García Márquez with reviving Latin American literature. Why is this? Research the changes in Latin American literature from the 1920s through the 1980s and make reference to Márquez's contributions.

- Critics have called García Márquez a master of the literary genre magical realism. What is magical realism? Where and how did it originate? Compare and contrast this Latin American genre with other genres or styles, such as science fiction/fantasy or prose poetry.

- García Márquez refers to "the civil wars," particularly when he introduces Santiago Nasar's father, Ibrahim. Investigate the political history of Latin America to determine whether this reference is fact or fiction. Write a paper supporting your findings.

- García Márquez is included in a group of writers referred to as the "Boom generation" in Latin America. Investigate Latin American culture to determine the following: Why do these writers have this distinction? When was the "Boom generation" prominent? Make a comparison to similar times and events in the United States' history, for example, the Harlem Renaissance.

- Investigate Latin American culture to gain an understanding of the idea of "male honor." What is the view of male image in Latin American culture today? How has this affected the treatment of women in Latin America?

Supernatural

Throughout of *Chronicle of a Death Foretold*, Márquez weaves elements of the supernatural. From the dreams that Santiago has the night before his death to the signs that people note foretelling his death, a sense of an unseen force prevails. For example, Santiago has inherited his "sixth sense" from his mother, Plácida. Margot feels "the angel pass by" as she listens to Santiago plan his wedding. Supernatural intervention pervades all aspects of the characters lives. For example, Purisima del Carmen tells her daughters that if they comb their hair at night, they will slow down seafarers.

Point of View

One of the most outstanding features of *Chronicle of a Death Foretold* is the point of view García Márquez uses to tell the story. Narrating the story from the first-person point of view is the unnamed son of Luisa Santiaga and brother of Margot, Luis, Jaime, and a nun. Having returned to the river village after being gone for twenty-seven years, the narrator tries to reconstruct the events of the day that ends in the murder of Santiago Nasar. Typically, a first-person narrator gives his own point of view but does not know what other characters are thinking: an ability usually reserved for the third-person omniscient, or all-knowing, point of view. In this novel, however, García Márquez bends the rules: the narrator tells the story in the first person, yet he also relates everything everyone is thinking.

Setting

Chronicle of a Death Foretold takes place in a small, Latin American river village off the coast of the Caribbean sometime after the civil wars. Once a busy center for shipping and ocean-going ships, the town now lacks commerce as a result of shifting river currents.

The events of the story evolve over a two-day time period. A wedding has taken place the night before between a well-known young woman from the town and a rich stranger who has been a resident for only six months. On the day of the murder, most of the townspeople have hangovers from the wedding reception. Because a visit from the bishop is expected, however, a festive air prevails.

Foreshadowing

Foreshadowing is typically achieved through an author's implication that an event is going to occur. García Márquez adds a twist to foreshadowing by telling exactly what is going to happen but not why it will happen. The entire story builds on the foretelling of Santiago's murder. The twins do not hide their plot; they tell everyone they meet of their plans. Each village person who hears about the scheme tells the next person. Santiago himself dreams of birds and trees the night before he dies, which his mother later interprets as the foretelling of his death. In the end, even Santiago knows that he is going to die.

Dream Vision

Throughout *Chronicle of a Death Foretold*, the characters refer to dreams and visions they have that are related to Santiago's impending death. Santiago's mother, for example, though well-known for her interpretations of dreams, fails to understand Santiago's dream of his own death. He tells her of his dream of traveling through a grove of trees and awakening feeling as if he is covered with bird excrement. She remembers later that she paid attention only to the part about the birds, which typically imply good health. Clotilde Armenta claims years after the murder that she thought Santiago "already looked like a ghost" when she saw him at dawn that morning. Margot Santiaga, listening to Santiago boast that his wedding will be even more magnificent than Angela Vicario's "felt the angel pass by." The author's many references to dreams and visions contribute to the surrealistic tone that is characteristic of magical realism.

Magical realism

Latin American culture gave birth to the literary genre magical realism. While critics attribute its beginnings to the Cuban novelist and short story writer Alejo Carpentier they agree that García Márquez has continued its tradition. The hallmark of magical realism is its roots in reality with a tendency toward the fantastic. That is, while everything a magic realist writes has a historical basis, it also has fictitious elements throughout. Emphasizing this point, García Márquez said in an interview with Peter H. Stone in *The Paris Review*, "It always amuses me that the biggest praise for my work comes for the imagination while the truth that there's not a single line in all my work that does not have a basis in reality."

The Birth of Latin American Culture

The term "Latin America" refers to the area that includes all of the Caribbean islands and the mainland that stretches from Mexico to the southernmost tip of South America. Latin America has a very long history, dating back to Columbus' discovery of the territory in 1492. Settled mostly by Spanish and Portuguese immigrants, Latin American culture is derived from both its European new-comers and its native inhabitants' traditions. Márquez blends elements from both cultures in *Chronicle of a Death Foretold*.

When the Spanish and Portuguese arrived, they easily overcame the native populations. The colonists destroyed native architecture, replaced the native religions with Catholicism, and strengthened the class system that already existed. As the natives died from diseases brought to them by the European immigrants, they were replaced by a new generation that resulted from an intermixing of the male immigrants and the female natives. The new population, known as mestizos, makes up the greatest part of Latin American society today. The mestizos, along with the remaining natives and African slaves, made up the lower class of Latin Americans. They and the mixed-blood mulattos worked as slaves or in the mines. The upper class included whites from Spain and Portugal known as peninsulares. The peninsulares were the only Latin Americans who could hold public office or work as professionals. Between the upper and lower class were the Creoles, European whites who were born in the colonies. The Creoles, although really equal to the peninsulares, were not permitted to hold government positions or to work as professionals. The struggles between the peninsulares and Creoles contributed to the wars for independence.

Colombian Civil Wars

In *Chronicle of a Death Foretold*, Ibrahim Nasar comes to the village after the end of the civil wars. The wars to which García Márquez refers are the Colombian wars for independence. Colombia, called New Granada at the time, experienced a separatist movement in the 1700s as a result of taxation and political and commercial restrictions placed on the Creoles. While independence was assured with Simon Bolivar's victory at the Battle of Boyaca, disagreement between Conservatives and Liberals arose over the issue of separation between church and state. Conservatives stood for a strong centralized government and the continuation of traditional class and clerical privileges. The Liberals believed in universal suffrage and the complete separation of church and state. The conflicts have continued throughout the years.

Post-Colonial Latin America

By 1830, most of the Latin America colonies had gained independence from their mother countries. While they continued to trade with Spain, Portugal, and Great Britain, they began to establish themselves as exporters of raw materials to the rest of the world. In addition to experiencing economic growth, Latin America also gained population. Immigrants poured into Latin American from less prosperous or politically unstable European countries. The growth in population and economic development has continued through the twentieth century. In the late 1990s, the Latin American economy was about the same size as the economies of France, Italy, or the United Kingdom.

Latin American Literature

Latin American literature aligns itself with the history of the region. Literary experts typically delineate four periods of Latin American literature: the colonial period, the independence period, the national consolidation period, and the contemporary period. During the colonial period, the literature reflected its Spanish and Portuguese roots and consisted primarily of didactic prose and chronicles of events. The independence movement of the early 1800s saw a move towards patriotic themes in mostly poetic form. The consolidation period that followed brought about Románticism—and later, modernism—with essays being the favorite mode of expression. Finally, Latin American literature evolved into the short story and drama forms that matured in the early twentieth century. The mid-twentieth century saw the rise of magical realism, for which García Márquez is best known. García Márquez was part of the "boom" trend, the growth of novel writing, that occurred in the 1960s and 1970s. During the boom trend, male voices and masculine themes dominated Latin American writing. Recently, female writers have been recognized for their early works as well as their current achievements.

Critical Overview

Critics credit García Márquez with bringing attention to Latin American literature. When García Márquez first appeared on the literary scene with his popular *One Hundred Years of Solitude*, reviewers praised not only his style but also his ability to tell a story to which everyone can relate. According to John Sturrock in the *New York Times Book Review*, García Márquez is "one of the small number of contemporary writers from Latin America who have given to its literature a maturity and dignity it never had before." David Streitfeld adds this sentiment in the *Washington Post*, "More than any other writer in the world, Gabriel García Márquez combines both respect (bordering on adulation) and mass popularity (also bordering on adulation)." Following on the success of this first novel, García Márquez has continued to build his reputation as a writer and storyteller.

By the time Jonathan Cape Limited of London published the English translation of *Chronicle of a Death Foretold* in 1982, García Márquez had established himself as a master of magical realism, a literature genre born in Latin America. Magical realism, a unique blending of fantasy and reality, evolved out of a culture that has been shaped by a combination of ethnic and religious populations that practice animism, voodoo, and African cult traditions. García Márquez credits his life experiences and his heritage with his ability to present the magical as part of everyday life. He says in a *UNESCO Courier* interview with Manuel Oscorio, "the area is soaked in myths brought over by the slaves, mixed in with Indian legends and Andalusian imagination. The result is a very special way of looking at things, a conception of life that sees a bit of the marvelous in everything."

Throughout García Márquez's long writing career, critics have commended his unique style. Besides his mastery of magical realism, García Márquez also possesses a talent for applying to his stories unconventional narrative styles, universal themes, and an unusual journalistic style that is often a commentary on social and political issues. *Chronicle of a Death Foretold* contains all of these. First, García Márquez has the narrator tell the story in the first person, but from an omniscient point of view. As Ronald De Feo says in a review in the *Nation*, "This narrative maneuvering adds another layer to the book." Next, the themes in *Chronicle of a Death Foretold* touch on universal concerns including male honor, crimes of passion, loyalty, and justice. Finally, most critics agree that *Chronicle of a Death Foretold* provides a snapshot in time of a society that remains captured by its own outmoded customs, beliefs, and stories.

While *Chronicle of a Death Foretold* retains a fairly widespread popularity, some reviewers have not been as accepting of its unusual form. The very characteristics of García Márquez's novel that most critics applaud have prompted others' scorn. Keith Mano, for example, says in the *National Review*, "In general, I wish García Márquez hadn't surrendered so many of the devices and prerequisites that belong to fiction: subjectivity, shifting POV, omniscience, judgment, plot surprise." Anthony Burgess has even harsher criticism in his review in *The New Republic*. He calls the book "claustrophobic" and goes on to say, "It does not induce a view, as better fiction does, of human possibilities striving to rise out of a morass of conservative stupidity. The heart never lifts. All that is left is a plain narrative style and an orthodox narrative technique managed with extreme competence. Perhaps one is wrong to expect more from a Nobel Prizeman."

Recognized for his revival of Latin American literature, García Márquez receives credit, too, for reinvigorating the modern novel genre. Overall, critics maintain that García Márquez deserves international acclaim for his unique style, plots, themes, and blending of fantasy and realism. In a review in *Tribune Books*, Harry Mark Petrakis describes García Márquez as "a magician of vision and language who does astonishing things with time and reality." Readers all over the world who await García Márquez's books would concur.

What Do I Read Next?

- Translated from Spanish to English in 1970, *One Hundred Years of Solitude* stands as García Márquez's best-known novel. It combines historical and fictional elements to tell the story of the rise and fall of a small, fictitious town—Macondo, Colombia. Many critics claim that while the novel reflects the political, social, and economic ills of South America, it actually depicts a more universal worldview.

- Many reviewers rate García Márquez's 1975 novel, *The Autumn of the Patriarch*, as his second-finest work. He attempts different stylistic techniques in this story of a political tyrant who has ruled for so long no one can remember his predecessor. García Márquez writes stream-of-consciousness-like sentences and uses a great deal of color and imagery to tell this tale.

- While the main character in *The Autumn of the Patriarch* lives in great isolation and never knows love, the main characters in *Love in the Time of Cholera* experience all kinds of love. Published in 1988, the book tells the story of star-crossed lovers who find themselves back together after over fifty years of separation.

- García Márquez writes about Simon Bolivar in his historical fiction, *The General in His Labyrinth*. This 1990 novel depicts General Bolivar, the liberator of Latin America, leaving for exile in the face of his former admirers' derision.

- Author Bill Boyd produced a nonfiction biography that reads like a novel with 1998's *Bolivar, Liberator of a Continent: A Dramatized Biography*. This accessible text tells the story of Simon Bolivar with both personal and political detail; Boyd also gives some attention to Bolivar's relationship with the United States.

- A rabid dog bites a nobleman's twelve-year-old daughter in García Márquez's *Of Love and Other Demons*. This 1995 story becomes more complicated when an exorcist falls in love with the girl.

- Another author who has successfully combined magical realism with historical detail and political commentary is Isabel Allende. Her 1982 debut novel (first published in the United States in 1985) *The House of Spirits* tells the story of a Chilean family through multiple generations, touching on themes of pride, class, power, sexuality, and spirituality.

Sources

Alonso, Carlos, "Writing and Ritual in *Chronicle of a Death Foretold*," in *Gabriel Garcia Marquez: New Readings*, edited by Bernard McGuirk and Richard Cardwell, Cambridge University Press, 1987, pp. 151-68.

Berg, Mary G., "Repetitions and Reflections in *Chronicle of a Death Foretold*," in *Critical Perspectives on Gabriel Garcia Marquez*, edited by Bradley A. Shaw and Nora Vera-Godwin, Society of Spanish and Spanish-American Studies, 1986, pp. 139-56.

Burgess, Anthony, review in *The New Republic*, Vol. 188, No. 1, May 2, 1983, p. 36.

Christie, John S., "Fathers and Virgins: Garcia Marquez's Faulknerian *Chronicle of a Death Foretold*," *Latin American Review*, Vol. 21, No. 41, June, 1993, pp. 21-29.

De Feo, Ronald, review in *Nation*, December 2, 1968.

Elnadi, Bahgat, Adel Rifaat, and Miguel Labarca, "Gabriel García Márquez: The Writer's Craft," interview in *UNESCO Courier*, February, 1996, p.4.

García Márquez, Gabriel, in an interview with Claudia Dreifus, in *Playboy*, February, 1983.

Gass, William H., "More Deaths Than One: *Chronicle of a Death Foretold*," *New York*

Magazine, Vol. 16, No. 15, 11 April, 1983, pp. 83-4.

Grossman, Edith, review, in *Review*, September/December, 1981.

Mano, Keith, review, in *National Review*, Vol. 35, No. 2, June 10, 1983, p. 699.

Millington, Mark, "The Unsung Heroine: Power and Marginality in *Chronicle of a Death Foretold*," *Bulletin of Hispanic Studies*, Vol. 66, 1989, pp. 73-85.

Petrakis, Harry Mark, review, in *Tribune Books*, April 17, 1988.

Sheppard, R. Z., review, in *Time*, March 16, 1970.

Stone, Peter H., interview, in *Paris Review*, Winter, 1981.

Streitfeld, David, review in *Washington Post*, October 22, 1982.

Sturrock, John, review in *New York Times Book Review*, September 29, 1968.

Yardley, Jonathan, review in *Washington Post Book World*, November 25, 1979.

For Further Study

Bell-Villada, Gene H., *García Márquez: The Man and His Work*, University of North Carolina Press, 1990.

> Followed by an extensive bibliography, this book puts Márquez in the company of other authors whose readers appreciate their ability to combine the commonplace with pioneering philanthropic political trends.

Donoso, Jose, *The Boom in Spanish American Literature*, translated by Gregory Kolovakos, Columbia University Press, 1977.

> While this author asserts that the term "the Boom Generation" is misleading, he acknowledges that the novels and novelists coming out of the period deserve their notoriety. In addition, Donoso explains the origin of the term.

Gonzalez Echevarria, Roberto, *Myth and Archive: A Theory of Latin American Narrative*, Cambridge University Press, 1990.

> Echevarria provides an extensive bibliography from which he has culled his ideas for his theory of how and where the Latin American

narrative started and how it fits in
with the modern novel.

Gabriel García Márquez and the Powers of Fiction,
edited by Julio Ortega, University of Texas Press,
1988.

A book of critical essays on the
works of Gabriel García Márquez,
this collection provides insight on
Márquez's style through various
scholars' viewpoints.

Landmarks in Modern Latin American Fiction,
edited by Philip Swanson, Routledge [and] Kegan
Paul, 1990.

The "Boom" period in Latin
American literature provides the
backdrop to this compilation of
essays that pertain to key texts
written during the era.

Martin, Gerald, *Journeys Through the Labyrinth:
Latin American Fiction in the Twentieth Century*,
Verso, 1989.

Beginning with the 1920s and
continuing through the 1980s, the
author presents a view of Latin
American literature seen through the
perspective of themes and historical
periods. He presents new works and
authors as well as a list of primary
texts and a critical bibliography.

Wolin, Merle Linda, "Hollywood Goes Havana:

Fidel, Gabriel, and the Sundance Kid," in *The New Republic*, Vol. 202, No. 16, April 16, 1990, p. 17.

> This article describes the internationally known Foundation for New Latin American Cinema and film school located in Cuba that are headed by García Márquez. The school receives contributions from such recognizable people as Robert Redford and offers the typical courses needed to learn the art and craft of filmmaking.

CPSIA information can be obtained
at www.ICGtesting.com
Printed in the USA
BVOW06s0214111017
497339BV00016B/103/P